MY SENECA VILLAGE

My Seneca Village

Marilyn Nelson

South Hampton, New Hampshire

Library of Congress Control Number: 2015905711

ISBN 978-1-60898-196-0 (hardcover: alk. paper)
ISBN 978-1-60898-197-7 (paperback: alk. paper)
ISBN 978-1-60898-198-4 (ebook)

ACKNOWLEDGMENTS

My thanks to the New York City Historical Society, and
to Rev. Richard Allen, Andres Blackwell, Regina Brooks,
Pamela Espeland, John and Mary Foley, Darin Keech, Peter
N. Nelson, Ann Perez, Elfriede Wilde, and Mary Williams.

Some of these poems appeared earlier in the online
journals *Drunken Boat, Mezzo Cammin,* and *New Haven
Poets,* 2nd Edition.

"The Cotillion" and "Tub-Men" are reprinted by permission
of *The Normal School,* c. 2008 by Marilyn Nelson.

www.namelos.com

My Seneca Village

Contents

Contents

Welcome to My Seneca Village

Seneca Village existed from 1825 through 1857. It was located between 82nd and 89th Streets and Seventh and Eighth Avenues in the Upper West Side area of New York City. Today, this area is part of Central Park. While it existed, Seneca Village was Manhattan's first significant community of African American property owners. By the 1840s, it had become a multiethnic community of African Americans, Irish and German immigrants, and perhaps a few Native Americans. According to the 1855 New York State Census, there were some 264 individuals living there. There were three churches. There was a school. There were several cemeteries. There were businesses. There were homes, with yards and gardens. There was an apple orchard. There were families. There were friends. There was happiness, there was grief. By 1857, everyone would have been forced to move, and Seneca Village would be completely erased by the creation of Central Park.

Central Park was America's first major landscaped public park. Frederick Law Olmsted and Calvert Vaux, the winners of the 1858 design competition for Central Park, along with other socially conscious reformers, understood that the creation of a great public park would improve public health and contribute greatly to the formation of a civil society. The state legislature authorized the City of New York to use the power of eminent domain to acquire more than 700 acres of land. The success of Central Park fostered the urban park movement, one of the great hallmarks of democracy of nineteenth-century America. And that is wonderful. Creating the park, however, required razing Seneca Village, which had been one of the city's most stable African American settlements, and displacing another roughly 1,600 poor residents, including Irish pig farmers and German gardeners, who lived in shanties nearby. To convert the swampy area into the park the designers had envisioned, several hundred thousand trees were planted, more than three million cubic yards of soil were moved, roads and bridges were constructed, and a large reservoir was dug out. Creating the park erased Seneca Village and its poor white neighbors, to be forgotten for one hundred thirty-five years.

Unlike today, when two minutes of googling yields all of what is known about Seneca Village, at the time when I leaped at the thought of learning about this fascinating corner of American history, the only way to learn the story was to go to a book called *The Park and the People: A History of Central Park* by Roy Rosenzweig and Elizabeth Blackmar (Cornell University Press, 1998), which gave the first historical account of Seneca Village, and to histories of the state, the region, and the nation. In 1997, the New York Historical Society opened an exhibition called "Before Central Park: The Life and Death of Seneca Village," which was based on that book. Grady T. Turner and Cynthia R. Copeland co-curated the exhibition, and Carol May and Tim Watkins of May & Watkins Exhibition Inc. were the designers.

As I read about the community and the monumental work of earth-moving and landscape design that swallowed it, the book that grew in my mind was a portrait of a community, a collection of individual portraits that converge to form a communal portrait. I re-read books of poems about communities: Langston Hughes' Harlem poems, Gwendolyn Brooks' "Bronzeville" poems, Sherwood Anderson's *Winesburg, Ohio*, Edgar Lee Masters' *Spoon River Anthology*, Dylan Thomas' *Under Milk Wood*. For several years I lived, with great delight, a sort of parallel existence, with characters I made up to fit the names and identifying labels I found in census records of Seneca Village. As I invented these characters and their world, I felt I was coming to know and love them. Some of them made me sad. Others made me laugh. With great pleasure, I introduce them to you.

—*Marilyn Nelson*

My Seneca Village

Broadway, 1825. Horse-drawn carriages, the legs of well-dressed men, the full long skirts of well-dressed women, all seen from the level of a bootblack bowed to industriously polish with a cloth the boot of a man (I'm thinking the man's pants are striped, and he's standing with one foot on the pavement and one foot lifted onto the shoe-shine box) who is holding a newspaper. Perhaps we can read a headline and a date. Though we see many people, we only see the face of the bootblack, Andrew Williams.

Land Owner
Andrew Williams, bootblack, 1825

There ain't nothing shameful about good, honest work.
It's a proud man that comes home with a decent wage.
I keep my head down. I listen when rich folks talk.
The finer the leather, the wiser the financial sage.

One foot on my box, Mister Man stands tapping The News
on his knee, talking shop confidentially with a friend.
I wipe off the filth, then, with a clean rag, smooth
his boot with lampblack, beeswax, and lanolin.

I deal merchandise shipped in on the Erie Canal.
Buy low, sell high. Then buy land, for the right to vote.
(You massage through his boot; caress his toes, his heel:
if you're lucky, he'll say what's coming on tomorrow's boat.)

Thanks to dropped tips, I'm a bootblack with his own place.
I may bow at their knees, shushing with the horsehair brush,
but I buff with spit on a rag to a mirrored face
aflame with pride, blazing like a burning bush.

Carrying the sign he puts up every day (the poem's title) down in the city, Epiphany Davis is standing in front of his little house. We see him from behind, so we see his house, and down the street other little houses, and perhaps one or two neighbors walking, or working in their gardens.

15¢ Futures
Epiphany Davis, 1825

I set up my cash box and my bones and cards
on Broadway, most days, offering what I see
of what's to come. For a donation, words
fall from my mouth, surprising even me.

Uncle Epiphany doesn't forecast death
or illness worse than gout or a broken bone.
The sailors stop. They listen with caught breath
as I tell them some girl's heart is still theirs alone.

(... or not. Young love is such a butterfly.)
Girls come, arms linked, giggling behind their fans.
The sad come. Uncle Epiphany does not lie.
I close shop, and come back up here to my land.

It's a new world up here, of beggar millionaires:
neighbors who know how we all scrimped and saved
to own this stony swamp with its fetid air,
to claim the dream for dreamers yet enslaved.

I'm Epiphany Davis. I am a conjure-man.
I see glimpses. Glass towers ... A horseless vehicle ...
An American President who is half African ...
Until you pay me, that's all I'm going to tell.

Diana Harding, a "traditionally built" woman dressed in a long full skirt and shirt, with her head wrapped in a kerchief, stands with one hand holding the handle of a shovel, the other wiping her face with a handkerchief. She's standing next to a newly planted sapling, behind which are several more saplings, enough to show us that she's planting an orchard. Perhaps we see a lane behind her, with a house or two, a neighbor or two.

Saplings
Diana Harding, 1826

Freed by a miraculous codicil,
I find myself the owner of one me,
two slightly swampy lots, one deeeep well,
one one-room palace, and opportunity.
In honor of generations denied the right to roots,
I plant saplings. We'll harvest the future's fruits.

Lots of faces, people of all ages, most of them
different shades of brown. (There might be one
or two sour-looking white men on the sidelines;
maybe some whites pointing and laughing;
some white children staring with open mouths.)
The parade takes place in the city, probably
on Broadway; we should know that from the
background buildings. We see the flag and
flag-bearers, the banners they carry, and one
or two bands. We might be able to recognize
Epiphany Davis in the scene. We see Obadiah
and Elizabeth. One of the banners says "SENECA
VILLAGE AFRICAN MUTUAL RELIEF SOCIETY,"
and some faces marching behind this banner will
be seen again later.

Across the Parade
Epiphany Davis, July 5, 1827

I glimpsed something today, at the parade
to celebrate our freedom. (Who were once
not even human.) Bass and snare drums made
Broadway reverberate, but I saw a glance ...

What a parade it was! Brown faces flowed
for blocks! (For the first time Old Glory flew
for us, too.) Sad excitement filled the crowd:
quiet, it owned the whole damn avenue.

Black institutions made their existence known
in six-inch letters painted on bright silk:
MOTHER BETHEL CHURCH A.M.E. ZION,
AFRICAN THEATRE COMPANY OF NEW YORK,

NY MANUMISSION SOCIETY, THE NY
AFRICAN FREE SCHOOL, MASONIC LODGE NO. 1,
PHILOMATHEAN LITERARY SOCIETY,
ABYSSINIAN DAUGHTERS OF ESTHER ASSOCIATION.

Behind the bands and banners, dignified rows
of brothers and sisters marched, straw-foot, hay-foot,
whose fraught, trail-blazing arcs I somehow know
(but never tell) from casting bone and root.

Brown people, in neat, homemade uniforms,
plumed tricorns, the Grand Marshall on his horse:
what a beautiful race of unicorns!
(I see, but can't change, our self-losing course.)

I saw Obadiah McCollin and Elizabeth
Harding (Sis Harding's girl—the one that reads)
exchange a look that said I Do Till Death,
from opposite curbs of the surging, life-filled street.

We recognize some of the faces at this meeting,

which takes place in one of the churches we will

see again later. The sign from the parade is tacked

up on the wall. Levin Smith is standing, and the

others are seated. It's clear from their clothing

that these are poor people. Maybe someone has

a hole in the bottom of his boot. Maybe some are

wearing clothes with patches.

African Mutual Relief Society
Levin Smith presiding

This meeting of the African Relief
Society is called to order. Brother Rich
will collect the dues while Miss Sara says the pledge.
Thank you. This month's expenses on behalf
of our members and neighbors facing grief,
illness, and poverty were minimal,
praise Jesus. No one died; everyone's well.

But we must stand prepared to stop the least
of us from being pushed from poverty
to begging, by sudden catastrophe.
Good servants repay more than they hold in trust:
let's find new ways our talents may be increased.
Guided by peace, order, friendship, and good will,
let's think beyond another sweet potato pie sale!

In the Colored School, in a church basement: one large room, wooden beams overhead, four or five tables at each of which two or three children are seated, working on slates. The teacher, a handsome young brownskin woman, is speaking, holding something she's showing them and teaching about. A few children's drawings are on the wall. Freddy is at one of the tables, elbow on table, cheek on fist, gazing out the window. We see what he's seeing: a squirrel in a tree and some of the village houses.

Too Light for Gravity
Frederick Riddles, ca. 1826

A blue knitted cap hides the cockles of his hair.
A thick striped sweater hides him from ears to butt.
His mittens match his cap (clearly mother-knit).
Short pants, tall socks, a down-at-the-heels pair

of ankle-high black boots. His lunch and slate
are strapped together. Shooter and aggies clink
in his right-front pocket. In his right-rear pocket a sling.
In his cerebral cortex a fireworks of thought.

What's "God," anyways? And how does God decide
who's rich and who's a slave, who's white, who's black?
Why don't other people think what I think?
Do white people bleed a different color blood?

Can something be too light for gravity?
Since I was born free, do I own myself
the same as Mama and Papa own themselves?
If you don't own nothing, what's the point of being free?

Why don't the stars fall down? Did Adam name
the numbers? How far? Frederick is late,
as usual. He slides into his seat,
his gaze caught by the world in the window-frame.

Freddy is a small silhouette standing outside

in front of a house, looking up. Through the

windows of this house and the windows of nearby

houses we see the light from lanterns or candles.

The vast, starry night sky overhead.

Under the Fathomless
Frederick Riddles, ca. 1828

Am I the only person that dreams my dreams?
Does anybody else on this planet think my thoughts?
Are my ideas like darting lights I've caught?
Is my mind a net sieving through thought-filled streams?

Frederick thinks his way through recess, while
the other boys play rolley-hole and catch,
the girls chant palm slap, or jump double-dutch:
lost in the moment of being a child.

He wonders, half-listening to the rhyme,
whether there is, somewhere, a Mary Mack,
and who buttons the buttons on her back.
If there's eternity, then what is time?

How do we know everyone is unique?
Who except God is able to compare
all of us? What if there's a boy somewhere
whose Self and mine are perfectly alike?

What would that mean? Would it make my life less
than what I know it is when I watch clouds
form and dissolve, or when I am allowed
to stand at night under the fathomless.

Inside the Riddles house, Angelina sits at the rough table, with one or two other adults. They hold slates. Freddy is standing in front of them, teaching.

Gradual Emancipation

Angelina Riddles, 1827

Sometimes my Freddy comes home in such a fever
it's all we can do to get him to settle down
for lessons, he's so het-up with whatever
new thought has fallen on his fertile ground.

By state law born free, but by law indentured,
to be legally freed only at twenty-one,
I grew gradually free. But I remained unlettered
until I became the student of my son.

I'm becoming quite the lady. I can write A,
which is what my name begins with. Ignorance
may be a shackle, but I'm freer every day.
And wiser, if such a word can describe a dunce.

For most of my twenty-nine years I've been *free-but-not-free.*
This is a *contradiction*, I now know.
But it's *universal, metaphorically.*
I suddenly understand. With an oh of awe.

*The 1799 New York State Act for the Gradual Abolition of Slavery
declared that, from July 4 of that year, all children born to parents
enslaved in the state of New York would be free. However, the Act
held that the children would be required to serve their mother's owner
until age twenty-eight for males, and age twenty-five for females. The
law thus defined the children of slaves as a type of indentured servant,
while scheduling them for eventual freedom. The last slaves in New
York State were emancipated by July 4, 1827.*

We recognize Elizabeth from "Across the Parade,"
only now she's big with child. She's sitting in a
chair in Sarah's kitchen while Sarah braids her
hair. Her hair is half-finished: half braided, half
wild. Sarah's mouth is open: she's clearly a Yenta.
Around them, handmade furniture, whitewashed
clapboard walls, herbs hanging to dry, several
pottery jars with cork stoppers. A pottery salt
container hangs on the wall next to the wood-
fired cook stove. Maybe another woman is sitting
there, waiting her turn.

Sky-Land
Sarah Matilda White, 1831

Elizabeth, that bump looks good on you!
Don't blush, honey. Love is a joy to share.
Now, what are we doing today with that mop of hair?
Sit on down. I'll fetch warm water and shampoo.

This week: shagbark nut oil with peppermint.
Mortar and Pestle and I are on a quest
to find which combinations work the best,
kettle by kettle of crushed oil and scent.

You heard about Jane Bolden? Such a shame.
Lean back. But she was lustful to the end!
Acted like every man was her boyfriend.
Sometimes I was tempted to call her out of her name.

Pat dry, while I heat the oil. You heard about
that Nat Turner, that led slaves to rebel?
For two days whites in Virginia lived in hell
on earth like us, I hear. Yes, mad: no doubt.

Thinking justice means turning the tables around,
showing the cruel no mercy. That makes sense
by the natural logic of experience,
but it ain't the teaching my mama passed down.

Alright, Elizabeth: cornrows again?
You're too tender-headed, girl. Try not to flinch!
Fifty-five they killed, for which hundreds were lynched.
Yes, he was a hero; a man among men.

He was hanged, flayed and quartered; they cut off his head.
Maybe God spoke. Maybe madness played a part.
But I believe vengeance harms the avenging heart.
Was he right or wrong? Ask the future. Ask the dead.

All done! Tell Obadiah to watch his back ...
Thanks! Have a nice day! Yes, that's on my list
of things to ask, when I'm called to my rest
in that sky-land where everybody's black!

*In November, 1831, enslaved visionary Nat Turner led a well-planned
revolt in Virginia.*

Charlot Wilson sits beside someone's sickbed. The sick person is grayish, with sunken eyes and cheeks. Charlot looks like a rose-cheeked, brown Florence Nightingale.

Bring Out Your Dead
Charlot Wilson, 1832

Over the course of a day the eyeballs sink
into their sockets; there are muscle spasms,
diarrhea. Soon the entire organism
curls up and dies, with a pestilential stink.

Could be something in the air ... In the water we drink?
... Salt and molasses. A lump of camphor gum
in a bag tied around the neck. Jamaican rum ...
And still they purge. Helpless, we watch them shrink.

The wealthy escape to the countryside.
The poor have to inhale the city's breath
fusty with horses, pigs, latrines, and death.
It's easy to predict who will live, who will die.

Some preach that plagues are God's just punishment
for intemperance. The McCollins's baby fell
ill with the cholera, too. His fontanel
sank in, his crying stopped. He was innocent.

He died without knowing discouragement
or wonder, and was buried the same day,
swaddled in white. Now the Front-Teeth-Missing play
"cholera," a game ending in lament.

*Four thousand people died in the 1832 New York City cholera epidemic,
caused by (though no one understood it then, and many whites
believed the disease was carried by blacks) a polluted water supply.*

Matilda Polk, a lovely young high-yellow woman, stands on a street in Seneca Village. All of the other people are browner than she is. They are all going about their business. She's holding a shopping basket, blushing. Three or four young men are flirting with her

The Yellow Girl
Matilda Polk

In me, peoples who hate each other met,
the lamb and lion lay down side by side,
setting aside her powerlessness, his might
just long enough to become mate and mate
and make me ivory-skinned and ebony-eyed.

We're in Sarah's kitchen again. The woman whose hair she is braiding looks very shocked, her eyes round, her hand over her open mouth.

The Park Theatre
Sarah Matilda White, ca. 1833

You heard what happened to Elizabeth
and Obadiah a few nights ago?
You know how crazy Elizabeth is for books.
Yes, I love it, too, when she reads to the Ladies Aid
from her pages-missing hand-me-down library.
How she'll close her eyes and repeat some plummy passage
sighing with such pleasure, you want to cry.

Hold your ear down. Well, they went to *Richard III*
at the Park Theatre. An anniversary treat.
Their love seems sweeter since they lost the child.
She said it hurt to see him humble himself
at the ticket window, offering a week's pay
to be seated in the highest balcony,
reserved for elite colored folk, and whores.

Frankly, I'd rather live without Shakespeare
than walk on the seamy side of the street.
But Obadiah will do anything
she asks. And she loves herself some Shakespeare!
Said she was whirled into a spell when the curtain rose
and Junius Booth spoke words she recognized,
in an accented voice she strained to hear.

She was so entranced by the tiny distant drama
that, when one of the pleasure-purveyors gave a cry
of release, Elizabeth woke up with a start.
She looked around the industrious balcony,
and burst out sobbing. Obadiah took her home
to the tenderness of wordless poetry,
she called it. Sweeter than Shakespeare, she said.

There's a crowd outside of the downtown theater, where the marquee announces a performance of Shakespeare's *Richard III* featuring the renowned colored tragedian, James Hewlett. Dressed-up black people are running out of the theater, chased by jeering, poorly-dressed white people; some whites on the street carry signs saying things like "No Shakspeare for N.....s" and "No N..... Kings!" In the midst of the chaos, Elizabeth, nine months pregnant, is punching a white ruffian in the eye as Obadiah tries to pull her away. In the background, a horse-drawn streetcar approaches.

The Shakespeare Riot
Sarah Matilda White, ca. 1834

Yes, those girls up at Prudence Crandall's school
in lily-white small-town Connecticut
are so brave, facing down angry white folks!
Living with white folks is like being married to
an unpredictable violent man
who explodes if an eggshell crunches under your feet.

You heard about the Anti-Shakespeare riot
at the African Grove Theatre's *Richard III*?
Did you know Elizabeth and Obadiah were there?
They'd hired James Hewlett, the famous black tragedian,
to head an all-black cast. Elizabeth
shouldn't have gone so far, she was so big,
but she said she had to see how the play ends.

"Imagine: a theatre where respectable colored families
can float on the blue cloud thrill of poetry,"
she said. She was holding the baby. I was braiding her hair.
She talked about Richard, "twisted, unloved,"
"the bitter villainy behind his charm,"
how he "connived his way up to the throne."

When whites broke in—No Shakespeare for naggers!—
a melee "in defense of poetry"
followed. They beat James Hewlett to a pulp.
Elizabeth blackened one white man's eye
before Obadiah wrestled her away
to the express four-horse streetcar uptown.

We're in the house of a poor but striving family. A basket and some unpacked goodies are on the table. Ada stands with one hand on her hip, the other holding a beautiful frothy lace petticoat. Charlotte is walking toward the doorway, her head thrown back, her nose in the air.

Hand-Me-Down Petticoat
Ada Thompson, ca. 1835

Traveling with large parcels at my age
takes a strong back. And there's always the risk—
given my long walk home through the woods past dusk—
that some man may see me as his privilege.

But one weekend a month, I take that chance.
After a month spent virtually alone—
silent, invisible—in Babylon,
I'm home. And you give me this arrogance?

I brought home half a loaf of store-bought bread,
a slice of ham, some cheese ... And you still pout,
as if second-hand honey isn't sweet.
Who put such prideful thoughts into your head?

Now, listen, Girl: this hand-me-down petticoat
is beautiful! It just needs to be cleaned.
Miss Astor's so generous! Yes, it is stained,
but poor people give thanks for what we get!

It's a little too long, but it only needs a hem.
I'll take the waist in; it will be just fine.
You're lucky to have a petticoat at thirteen.
Pride goeth before a fall. And so doth shame.

You say you'd rather wear tow-cloth? That slaves
labored over this cotton? Well, my girl,
so did your mama. Wake up to the world:
a colored girl can't be so sensitive!

One girl refusing a cast-off petticoat
won't part the bloody sea of history.
Refusing it won't make nobody free!
Now, wash your face. Sit down, sweet darling. Eat.

We recognize the church: the Mutual Relief

Society meeting took place here. We recognize

some of the village individuals in the church, as

the men lock the doors and stand guard, while

women and children sit or lie in the hand-hewn

pews. Fear is in the air.

Wild Night
Rev. Christopher Rush, 1835

The white folks were restless again last night.
All we could do was keep the faith, and wait.
My first parishioners started arriving at sunset,
having heard rumors, and reluctant to stay at home.
Our shadows danced in the sanctuary's candle-flames
as audible whiffs of pandemonium
drifted to us, like smoke from distant fires.
With most of the village in, I locked the doors.

I asked everyone to bow their heads and pray.
Pray for this nation's struggle to be free
for ALL Americans. Equality
must be bitter, if you've always been on top,
and you're slapped awake out of a lifelong sleep.
Pray we'll pull together toward a common hope.

> *... Hundreds of voices raised.*
> *Could that be drums?!*
> *That was a firehouse bell ...*
> *That was a scream!*

Near dawn. The children and some mothers sleep;
roosters crow morning, a couple of yard-dogs yap,
the songbirds choir. The violence has stopped.
I step out into every day new light.
My little flock has weathered a wild night.
But someone somewhere is less fortunate.
Tim Seaman comes out, nods, and finds a tree.
Would every now held such tranquility.

There were many anti-abolition riots in New York City in 1834–45.
White mobs attacked targets associated with abolitionists and African
Americans. People were beaten. More than seven churches were
damaged, many of them belonging to African American congregations.

It's dusk, during a blizzard. Snow blows

horizontally. Beyond the trees, in the far distance,

the sky is red. We're in a crowd of bundled-up

village people, of all ages. Some are holding

hands. Plez stands behind Susan, with his arms

around her.

Fire, Ice, Kiss
Susan and Pleasant Smith, December 16, 1835

Stomping our ice feet, we shivered in layered shawls,
kerchiefs and coats, shoulders hunched to our ears.
The night sky glowed red with reflected fire.
Wind-whirls brought snatches of faraway clangs and calls.

Some people prayed, or blew into mittened fists.
Some said it served them fat cats right, and laughed.
They danced with bitter joy on the snowdrifts,
spectators of distant apocalypse.

Drawing me into a puffy embrace,
Plez said, *Hell's furnace for men who catch fugitive slaves.*
Are there twenty righteous people down there to save?
He pulled me close. *Come here, sweet pillar of ice!*

*Some 700 buildings in the business district of Manhattan burned to
the ground on this frigid night. Firefighters tried to put out the fires
with water pumped from the river, but the water froze in the fire hoses.*

We recognize Plez. It's late at night, in an alley in a high-toned part of the city. There's a horse-drawn wagon to haul the tubs of sewage to be dumped into the river. Men wearing cloths tied over their faces carry full and empty buckets. Lanterns hanging from the wagon provide the only light. Some liquid splashes on the street. A couple of barking dogs.

Tub-Men
Pleasant Smith, 1837

Joseph, Alonzo, Neptune, Truss, and me
lit out under a sky paling towards dawn
yesterday, to trek on down into town
and take our places in the national economy.

Because times are tough all over, poverty
and unemployment rife. Who can compete
with immigrants who'll work for a bite to eat?
We're free now: ain't giving up our dignity.

It ain't like we've done day labor all our lives:
Joseph was a waiter, Neptune chopped firewood,
Truss had him a barber shop, when times were good.
It's a struggle, now, to feed our children and wives.

But there's always been work for men who will haul and lift,
doing the labor once reserved for slaves.
(It's ironic, that those who sweat over harvest have
—after the rich are served—so little left.)

By midmorning the corner crowd had thinned,
as men were picked. At noon, the only job
still open was emptying latrine tubs.
Am I a tub-man? I looked at my friends.

We thought the same thought. Our eyes wouldn't meet.
Have I fell so low? We trekked back to town last night.
Each took a barking alley by starlight.
And we emptied the perfumed privies of the elite.

Gray-haired, stooped Nancy Morris leans on a cane, holding open the trapdoor in her kitchen floor for a ragged, hungry-looking family of escaped slaves.

Conductor
Nancy Morris, widow, ca. 1838

When did my knees learn how to forecast rain,
and my hairbrush start yielding silver curls?
Of late, a short walk makes me short of breath,
and every day begins and ends with pain.
Just yesterday I was raising my girls;
now I'm alone, and making friends with death.

So let the railroad stop at my back door
for a hot meal. What do I have to lose?
The Lord has counted the hairs on my head
and made a little space under my floor.
All I ask of life is to be of use.
There'll be time to be careful when I'm dead.

Birth is a one-way ticket to the grave:
I've learned that much slowly, over the years,
watching my body age. Time is a thief,
and what we give away is all we can save.
So bring on the runaways! I know no fear.
Let life have meaning, if it must be brief.

*The Underground Railroad, a secret network of routes leading from
the South to freedom in Canada, operated from ca. 1801 to 1865.
People who risked their lives to help slaves escape on this route were
called "conductors."*

Angelina Morris is Nancy's daughter. We're on the street in front of Nancy's house. We can see other houses and gardens. Angelina is just about to step into the rented, livery-driven carriage on the arm of fancy-dressed Tim Seaman, but Nancy is there at her feet with a needle, making a few more stitches in the hem of Angelina's gown.

The Cotillion
Angelina Morris, 1844

Mama made my gown of Swiss muslin gauze
over satin, with matching satin trim,
tiny pleats at the waist, a rouleau hem,
and modest front and back décolletés.

Long kidskin gloves. A shawl of Belgian lace.
In my embroidered bag, a Spanish fan.
My hot-combed hair at my nape in a bun,
curling-iron curls on each side of my face.

Tim hired a liveried carriage for the night.
He wore a tailcoat, brought me a corsage.
(We earn good money now, so we can splurge,
this once, pretending we're rich socialites.)

In petticoats, ribbons, and ostrich plumes,
with watch chains, snuff boxes, and monocles,
we were enchanted individuals
last night, Cinderellas without our brooms.

The ballroom looked elegant, and the band
played waltzes and quadrilles. Colored New York
danced in its finery, forgetting work,
insult, and slavery still in our land.

1844 was the beginning of a period of national financial prosperity.

In the same church we've seen before, a small audience, some of whom we might recognize (Sarah is there, and Obadiah, and Freddy and Angelina Riddles, and others). Mrs. Stewart is speaking from the pulpit, pounding her fist into her palm.

Address

Delivered by Mrs. Maria W. Stewart (1803–1879), ca. 1845

Do the sons of Africa have no souls?
Do they feel no ambition? No desires?
Can a slave not be noble? A master be a fool?

Shall the earth be inherited by the fierce?
Shall ignorance continue to enchain
the ignorant, so their ignorance grows worse?

Shall we always be judged the lesser men?
Are we not equally able to achieve?
Not statesmen, scientists, historians?

Have we no heroes, gallant, fearless, brave?
No lecturers on natural history?
Are the distinguished extinguished by being enslaved

in this nation of freedom and democracy?
Lord, Ethiopia stretches her hands to Thee!

*Essayist, lecturer, abolitionist, and women's rights activist, Maria
Stewart was the earliest known American woman, and the first
African American woman, to lecture in public on political themes
and to leave copies of her texts. Her first publication, a twelve-page
pamphlet titled "Religion and the Pure Principles of Morality"
(1831), revealed her distinctive style, a mix of political analysis and
religious exhortation.*

Same church, similar scene. Mrs. Stewart is

raising her fist. A much larger audience. Some are

raising their fists as well.

Babylon

Address delivered by Mrs. Maria W. Stewart, ca. 1846

Like the great ancient city of Babylon,
America has boasted in her heart,
"I shall see no sorrow, for I am The Queen!"

She has turned herself into an open mart
where the biggest sellers are human bodies and souls,
and where people clamor to buy ugly art.

In one hand the reins, the other grasping the wheel
of government and power, she hawks the wine
of fornication, nations under her heel.

But by His Name, who sitteth on the throne,
the day comes, when the children of Africa shall rise!
When vice and immorality shall be put down!

The ear of the Lord is not deaf to our cries.
Our suit has reached the court of the Most High!

It's dusk. Margaret Cavanaugh, a shawl over her head and her bony shoulders, arranges patched blankets and coats over the two beds in the room. There are four children in each bed, ages 2, 3, 4, 6, 7, 8, 9, and 11. Through the window, her skinny husband can be seen shaking hands with a couple of the neighbors who have come to welcome them with sweet potato pies.

Counting Blessings
Joseph and Margaret Cavanaugh, ca. 1847

There's Bridget and Michael and Catherine and Ann,
there's Francis X., Moira, Theresa, and Sean:
none of them shivering, everyone fed,
head to feet sleeping, four butts to a bed.

*The 1845 Irish potato crop failure resulted in widespread famine.
More than one million Irish people—one out of every nine—died.
Hundreds of thousands emigrated to England, Scotland, and the
New World. Mortality rates of up to 30% were common on the
"coffin ships" crossing the Atlantic.*

In church. Charlotte Thompson, Ada's daughter

(from the "Hand-Me-Down Petticoat" poem) is

grown up now. We recognize her, in her wedding

dress. And we recognize Tim Seaman, who

used to date Angelina Morris. He might even be

wearing the same suit he wore to the cotillion. We

recognize many of the wedding guests. Elizabeth

and Obadiah have a couple of small children.

Thompson and Seaman Vows,
African Union Church
ca. 1847

Miss Charlotte Thompson, daughter of Ada
Thompson of Seneca and the late John,
and Timothy James Seaman, son
of the late Nancy Seaman, on Sunday.
Reverend Rush performed the ceremony.
The bride (24) was educated
by a literate friend, and by seeing
the African Theatre Company's
productions of *Macbeth* and *Richard III*.
She teaches in Colored School #3.
Her father was a slave. Her mother, freed
by a clause in her late mistress's will,
sews and sells exquisite lace lingerie.
The bridegroom (26) cannot read or write,
but ciphers and is a skilled carpenter.
His mother was slaved to an early death.
She told him he was descended from kings.

Freddy Riddles is grown up now, too. He's on
the deck of a sailing ship, dressed as a mariner,
but sitting with a pencil to write a letter to the
sweetheart he calls "Tildie," who is Matilda Polk,
the girl we met in "The Yellow Girl."

New York to Nicaragua
Frederick Riddles to Matilda Polk, July 24, 1848

Sailing choppy coastal waters. Seasick.
Nothing but blue to see, both sea and sky.
Our wooden vessel crackled, banged, and creaked.
Twenty awe-making sunrises and sunsets.

We followed Captain's orders: all hands on deck!
The glittering guidebook on the dome of stars.
Deep sea, long swells. The North Wind at our back.
One night, the long white ladder of moonlight.

Everything wet for days; no cut would heal.
Inland, the slave states blew soft winds off land.
Days grew warmer. We learned to read the skies.

We kept a watch at night for sleeping whales.
In storms, we set out buckets to catch rain.
(Tildie, I haven't forgotten your eyes.)

Frederick Riddles stands on the deck of a steamboat, on a tropical river. In the distance are the Nicaraguan twin volcanoes.

Nicaragua Crossing
Frederick Riddles to Matilda Polk, September 19, 1848

San Juan del Norte to San Juan del Sur:
the slim waist of the continent.
We steamed up the Rio San Juan.
Scenes my limited words can't paint.

The ancient fort, el Castillo,
on a green knob, forests behind.
San Carlos, where Lake Cocibolca
escapes down river to beyond.

What doesn't move is draped in vine.
And monkeys! Gaudily feathered birds!
I worked my way through Paradise!

On Ometepe Island, twin
volcanoes, their peaks wreathed in clouds ...
(But nothing rivaled your brown eyes.)

Matilda Polk is standing on the street in front of the general store/post office, gazing up after reading the postcard. We see the village around her, and various neighbors. A couple of white adults and children are also here.

Penny Postcard
Frederick Riddles to Matilda Polk, October 10, 1848

Landed in "Frisco."
Lodging at above address.
[Clumsy sketch of dolphin's leap.]
If words could dance!
                              Wait.

In the larger village church, more "high church,"

Episcopal. We're in the back of the church,

looking toward the pulpit. In the foreground we

see the backs of the heads of two little boys,

and a small raised fist: one of them is punching

the other. Their mother (maybe she's Angelina

Morris), sitting beside them, has turned toward

them with an angry face. In front of them we see

the backs of other people in pews. In the distance

we see Frederick Douglass in the pulpit.

Words and Whispers

Address delivered by Frederick Douglass (1803–1870), ca. 1848

A battle won is easily described;
the moral growth of a great nation requires
description and reflection, to be seen.

Hey, that's MINE!

A little learning is a dangerous thing;
the want of learning a calamity.

You better give it back!

The life of a nation can be secure
only while it is virtuous and true.

I MEAN it!

America has been false to the past,
false to the present, and solemnly binds
herself to be false to the future, too.

Give it back!

No harvest without plowing up the ground;
no rain without a rumble of dark clouds.

Oh, yeah?

It is easier to build strong children
than to piece back together broken men.

He started it!!

For he who sows the wind reaps the whirlwind.

Yessum.

Born enslaved in Maryland, Douglass is one of the most prominent figures in African American and American history. The "words" of this poem are his.

In the Episcopal churchyard, the black priest comforts the weeping parents: a thin young Irish girl wearing a shawl, and a gentle-looking black man holding his cap and embracing the girl. His family is there, in a cluster. Her parents stand at a distance, scowling, with their arms clenched.

Little Box
Reverend Walter Peters, All Angels' Church, November 18, 1849

Someone has died, who will never see the black
joylight expand in her mother's blue eyes.
Who will never grasp a pinky, nor be danced
up, down and around and lullabied all night.
Someone who will never come to realize
that her Dada's palms aren't dirty, they're just brown.
Who made HER mother, HIM father, then broke their hearts.
Who is their shooting star, glimpsed only once.
Someone who will never laugh, or play, or care ...

Praying that little box into the earth,
Rev. Peters asks forgiveness for his faint faith.
He thinks of the life of pain Someone was spared.

"A female still born child of Egbert Stairs (colored) & Catherine Cochran his wife (white) was buried in All Angels' churchyard, November 18, 1849"—from the church record.

Five tow-headed young men stand over a fresh

grave in the same churchyard. The bereaved

young parents of the previous poem are behind

them at a distance, putting flowers on their

child's grave. The youngest of the Donnelly

brothers is speaking to the others with great

passion.

Council of Brothers
James, John, Michael, Hugh, and Patrick Donnelly,
January, 1849

Our Mam, dead of fever, sleeps on the ocean floor.
Now cholera's took Dad. Listen to me:
all of our lives, we've been hungry and poor.
Well, I've had it up to here with poverty!
Laying awake every night with a growling gut,
wearing Hugh's smelly, outgrown, leaky boots.

Jamie's free, white, and almost twenty-one;
all of us have strong hearts and arms and backs;
I'm thirteen, but I'm strong as any man.
We are the orphans of the dispossessed.
What's to keep us from being rolling stones?

This morning, I hawked a headline hot off the press:
EXTRA! GOLD FOUND IN CALIFORNIA CREEK!
I say the Donnelly brothers should head west.

Back in the first church, the same one in which
the African Relief Society met. The minister
exhorting is the same minister who was locking
up the church in "Wild Night," only he's 15 years
older now. We recognize some of the villagers.

Miracle in the Collection Plate
Rev. Christopher Rush, 1850

Brothers and sisters, we know why we're here
this evening. The sad news has traveled fast
of Brother James's capture. For three years
he lived amongst us, tasting happiness.

His wife and child are here with us tonight.
God bless you, Sister. Without a goodbye,
James was handcuffed, and shoved on a steamboat
to Baltimore, to be sold—legally!

Neighbors, we know that upright, decent man:
James Hamlet: a loving husband, father, friend.
Many of us would gladly risk the fine
or prison sentence, if we could help him.

My friends, all is not lost! It's not too late!
We are told that Brother James may be redeemed!
His buyer will sell him! But we cannot wait:
we need eight hundred dollars to free him.

Eight hundred. I know every penny counts,
living from widow's mite to widow's mite.
But with God's help, we can raise that enormous amount!
Let's make a miracle in the collection plate!

*In 1850 the U.S. Congress passed the Fugitive Slave Law, which made
any federal marshal or other official who did not arrest an alleged
runaway slave liable to a fine of $1,000. Law enforcement officials
everywhere now had a duty to arrest anyone suspected of being a
runaway slave on no more evidence than a claimant's sworn testimony
of ownership. The suspected slave could not ask for a jury trial or testify
on his or her own behalf. In addition, any person aiding a runaway slave
by providing food or shelter was subject to six months' imprisonment
and a $1,000 fine. Officers who captured a fugitive slave were entitled
to a bonus. Slave owners only needed to supply an affidavit to a federal
marshal to capture an escaped slave. This law led to many free blacks
being conscripted into slavery, as they had no rights in court and could
not defend themselves against accusations. James Hamlet was the
first fugitive arrested under the new law. His African American and
Abolitionist friends raised the money necessary to purchase his freedom.*

Twelve or 15 men, of various ages and colors, hold up mugs of beer and sing together in a narrow, dark shebeen. We might recognize some of the men. Maybe a couple of the oldest Donnelly brothers are there. Mary is plump, 40-ish, wearing an apron, carrying stoneware mugs on a tray; James is behind a table, pouring from a stoneware pitcher into more mugs.

Cassidy's

James and Mary O'Neil Cassidy, ca. 1852

With just a little industry
a backyard tree becomes a chair.
With just a little energy
a board planed smooth becomes a bar.

With just a little elbow grease
tubers are transformed to poteen,
in chipped glasses promising peace
to working men, in our shebeen.

We greet their variegated faces:
friends fair, freckled, tan, and dark.
We pour for neighbors of both races,
thirsty after a day's hard work.

Sometimes a child comes for her dad,
but we don't serve drunks. We're a class
establishment. When someone's had
enough, we don't refill his glass.

Sometimes a man will raise a song
and all of us will sing along.
Sometimes a man weeps quietly,
and we pretend we do not see.

From one of the Seneca Village streets, we

look down at Jupiter Hesser, wild-haired, clearly

eccentric. He's wearing house slippers, trousers, a

plaid wool vest, and a top hat, and working in his

meticulous, fecund, sloping, perfectly beautiful

garden. It's spring. Below the garden is his

little German-style half-timbered house, where,

through an open door (we can read the sign—

the title of the poem—on the door), we can see

the grand piano and violin. There's a window next

to the door.

Professor Hesser, Music Lessons
Jupiter Hesser, Piano and Violin, ca. 1852

A painted shingle on the door. Within,
the larger of his ecstasy-machines
grins in its sleep, cradling the violin.
On the table: papers, his goose quill pen.

The slattern still abed. An open book
next to his side. The heirloom cuckoo clock
counts sieben. In the garden, long awake,
Jupiter stops weeding, and rests his back.

Da di di DUM! The tune which only he can hear
organizes the surf between his ears
in a sensible torrent. Notes cohere
like little dancing round black dots and spheres.

Kohlrabi, gooseberries, red cabbage, leeks …
The Chermany he left behind can lick
his hinter. Better to live among blacks
than to sell your soul to Schweinhund Catholics.

But he cannot understand the bigoted:
Some blacks are musicalisch talented.
Great music may grow in a woolly head.
If only they'd learn how to make black bread!

A citizen now, self-named Jupiter Zeuss
Thor Hesser, he calls all gods to serve his muse.
Who knows what symphonies we may produce,
which student take from us somethink of use?

*German immigrant Jupiter Zeuss Thor Hesser, a gardener and
composer, owned seven lots, which he called "Jupiterville," in Seneca
Village. He composed and published several popular songs.*

This is Sarah Matilda White again, but older.

She's still doing hair. And still talking.

Sisters of Charity
Sarah Matilda White, 1853

More Irish seem to arrive here every day,
like rats fleeing a ship that's going down.
Their women troll our streets for men at night;
their children run wild all day in shanty-town.

They come in coffin ships, with little more
than faith and hunger. Ignorant, unskilled,
they seem hell-bent on making themselves less,
like prodigal sons content to live in swill.

People who have nothing will rob the poor
to feed their children. Now I lock the house
and clutch my purse, as fearful as the rich.
They're starved of hope, desperate, and unwashed.

But I do like that flock of Irish nuns
who swoop like crows, catching truants by the ear
and marching them to school, then wake the tarts
to steer them toward respectable careers.

They are taking thousands of white fugitive slaves
who can't imagine better lives beyond
full stomachs, work, and a hovel called home,
and teaching them to dream of a free dawn!

The Irish famine refugees met with vehement racism from native-born American whites when they arrived in America. Many newspaper articles and cartoons depicted them as inferior to blacks. Father John Hughes (1797–1864), a fierce advocate of abolition and the rights of Irish immigrants, was the first Roman Catholic bishop, and then archbishop, of New York. He fought strenuously on behalf of the Irish, forcing reforms in the anti-Catholic public schools, inviting Roman Catholic religious orders to come to the city, and instituting a system of parochial schools (including four universities).

Professor Hesser's garden again, but later in the year. Different flowers, bigger plants. We're closer to the house now, but behind the boy. Boots with worn heels, socks falling down. Very Tom-Sawyer-ish in clothing. He's standing with one hand on either side of the doorframe, his head thrown back in ecstasy. Maybe we can read the sign on the door. The window next to the door is broken. Through the open doorway we see, perhaps, Hesser's hands on the piano. There's a homemade softball sitting on the piano.

The Deaf Boy
Marcus Smith, ca. 1852

All of a sudden the stickball game just stopped!
Most of the other boys scattered like shards.
My brother James pointed where the ball dropped,
somewhere deep in Professor Hesser's yard.
Moving his lips, James gestured with eyes and hands
that I was to go inside the Professor's fence.

Most of Seneca signals the Professor's mad,
finger-circling. He walks waving his arms.
I searched through his orderly garden's rows and beds,
ignored by robins taking a break from worms.
Perpetually hurrying and efficient bees
zigzagged, and aimless, tippling butterflies.

As I drew near the Professor's open door
every nerve in my body started shivering
as if a breath of January air
had scattered flurries on a clear day in spring.
I placed my hands on the doorframe. Our ball was laid
on top of the big black thing the Professor played.

He swayed, head back, eyes closed. He raised his brows
twiddling the far right side. Then all ten fingers
pounded the far left side as his face scowled.
And I was pulled through ecstasies and angers
by my hands' touch on the vibrating wood.
This is "MUSIC"! I thought. My whole being heard!

A group of about ten village children of various ages, playing in front of or behind a recognizable house or church or school. One of the older boys is Chris Tietjen, white, German. All of the other older children are black. There may be one or two other white children, but they are too young to play major roles. Chris is speaking to the combined group, gesturing with raised eyebrows.

Make-Believe
Christian Tietjen, ca. 1852

How come *you* get to be heroic slaves
crossing a river of ice floes to get free,
and *I* always have to be Simon Legree?

Why is it always *me* snapping the whip
while you flee screaming, or huddle in an embrace?
You make me feel like *I'm* in the wrong race!

Why don't *you* be the masters, for a change?
The game doesn't have to be always played the same.
Pretend *you* have no humility, no shame.

I'll be saintly, enslaved nobility,
and *you*, caving in to the red pitchforks of greed,
sell *me* down river, after promising I'd be freed.

C.W. Taylor's stage dramatization of Harriet Beecher Stowe's famous anti-slavery novel, Uncle Tom's Cabin, *was first performed in New York City at Purdy's National Theatre in 1852.*

Matilda Polk sits in a wagon loaded with all of her belongings, as the driver shakes the reins and clucks the horse to go. She has lost her youthful glow. She's looking back at the house. Other villagers, black and white, wave goodbye sadly, as they pack their own belongings into carts or wagons.

To Know
Matilda Polk, 1858

To know just how he suffered—would be dear—
    —Emily Dickinson

To know if, when, and where he breathed his last.
To know if his last word was my first name.
To know if some letters to me were lost.
To know if he lives: to know THAT, at least!

To know how long I must tend this guttering flame.

We've met Rev. Rush twice before. He's older now, but recognizable. He's in the pulpit of the new church. It's quite a bit larger. There are streamers and lots of flowers; the scene is very celebratory. Most of the congregation is black, but there might be a couple of white families, and maybe we see the couple whose baby died earlier, sitting in a pew with two or three biracial children. We should recognize several people. Everyone's dressed up. Maybe some of the women are fanning themselves. It's a hot August day.

Rejoice with Me

Rev. Christopher Rush, dedication of new church building,
New Hope Missionary A.M.E. Zion, August 4, 1853

Twenty-six years ago, at the parade
for New York State's Emancipation Day,
our five-year old was nowhere to be found.
Panicked, we searched the crowds, screaming his name.

We found him here at New Hope, waiting for us.
He didn't seem to think he had been lost:
he'd known where he was; he thought we must know, too.
All I could do was close my eyes and rejoice.

Jesus says God rejoices over each found sheep .
He rejoices when anyone returns to trust, to hope.
He kicks up his heels! He makes fresh lemonade!
He invites everyone to join in, to live it up!

Our new church building will offer welcome
To more sheep than could sit in the old one.
It enlarges our mission and our ministry.
Rejoice with me! Welcome to our new church home!

We have a new building! Rejoice with me,
in our sacred story of community:
in breaking ground together, raising a roof
with pennies and quarters. Rejoice with me!

The truest evidence that Jesus lives
is not a vacant grave, but fellowship;
not a stone rolled away, but a whole church
carried away, filled with the Christ spirit!

Brothers and Sisters, rejoice with me today,
for this spirit-filled church is carried away!
The risen Christ lives in our hearts and minds!
Rejoice! Rejoice! In the greatest of hope, I say:

Amen!

Some of the same village boys, about 11–14 years old. "Miz Harding's orchard" is the one she planted much earlier in the book, years ago, in the "Saplings" poem. By early morning light, the boys are scattering in the village streets, each headed toward his own home, clutching his stomach.

Sleep-Out

Kevin Cassidy, Charlie Hamlet, Marcus Smith,
"Teach" Tietjen, Elmo Wilson, ca. 1854

Pirates raided Miz Harding's orchard last night.
Silent, invisible in the darkness,
they filled their pockets with sweet gold treasures
and slid like shadows back into the gloom.

Pirates lit a fire, smoked cornsilk cigars.
They felt their faces blaze. They breathed harsh smoke.
They feasted on fragrant, fuzzy, firm fruit.
They took off their shirts and danced around the fire.

Pirates lay sleeping, lulled by the night's songs.
The day shift birds, each whistling its own tune,
began to warm up before dawn's first light.
Pirates woke to growling belly music.

They exchanged the secret pirate handshake,
then ran off, doubled over in self-hugs.
Staggering out of privies into homes,
pirates were boys in their mothers' embrace.

I had in mind a "take" on the famous Currier &

Ives prints of ice skaters in Central Park.

Pig on the Ice
Charlotte Seaman, ca. 1854

After the service, we dutiful few
followed the shouts and laughter to the pond.
All Seneca was out, even the new
German grocer and his four children, blond,
blue-eyed replicas of his ninth-month Frau,
with red cheeks. Brown ladies skated like swans,
crinolines billowing. Brave curliques
cut the smooth ice. Couples held mittened hands.
Runny-nosed brown and pink boys cracked the whip.
Above bare trees, clouds swept across the sky.
Then one of the Murphy's pigs decided to tip
after the children, slid, and flew sky-high!
Squealing its head off, it skidded and slipped,
toppling brown and white indiscriminately.

Nations of expletives sprang from our lips!

We see village houses we recognize, with "Condemned" signs on their front doors. Women are weeping. Some people are yelling. Some are folding their arms and shaking their heads. White men are shaking their fists at white cops who are nailing signs to doors. Black men are standing numb and powerless. This nonsense poem is made up of phrases taken from the New York State law of eminent domain.

The Law of Eminent Domain

"A very great number of poor families, who worked a number of years on these lots ... will be entirely ruined when they must give up their cultivated land and move away ... Please to have mercy on the Poor."
> —Jupiter Hesser, letter to New York Commission
> of Estimate, 1855

The appropriated property located
in the state of New York, pursuant to
paragraph ninety-seven of the state
finance law, notwithstanding the approved
appraisal herein vested, payable
subsequent to the jurisdiction claim,
shall advance without delay. The Comptroller shall
provide personal court order of the same.
Aforesaid deposit to furthermore
in subdivision (c) shall not comply
after the audit of the condemnor.
At any time failure to notify
shall be deemed an acceptance, and thereon
a valid waiver of transfer is withdrawn.

A handsome, white-haired, white bearded man with a Mona Lisa smile. Behind him, a fantasy tableau. From left to right: the first houses in the village, the later village, the destruction of the village, the work on the park (the thousands of workers brought in tens of thousands of tons of stone and topsoil, in horse-drawn wagons), the park, the contemporary sign in the park identifying the site of the former Seneca Village.

Uncle Epiphany
ca. 1855

Our African Ancestors always knew
a change was in the making: even then,
when each day was a cloud bank they flew through,
solid gray to the encircling horizon.
Had they not known how lucky we would be,
how could they go on? They trusted the sun
of life's infinite possibility
which they could not see, though they knew it shone.

Epiphanies appear, from time to time,
when I see through the cloud. This secret gift
ignites my eyes, and makes me smile and hum.
I am one who knows that time and we are mist
hiding Light's ever-changing panorama,
where the future holds a President Obama.

About the Poems

Even the casual reader will surely recognize the traditional poetic forms underlying most of these poems. Most of them are written in quatrains, the four-line rhyming stanzas ancient in the poetic traditions of Greece, Rome, and China, as well as the more modern traditions of European languages and those of the Middle East. Most of the poems we remember from childhood are written in quatrains, as are most of the poems we remember from later reading. There are various ways of rhyming the quatrain, the most common being abab (every other line rhymes) and abba (lines one and four rhyme, as do lines two and three). My quatrains in *My Seneca Village* use several different rhyme schemes.

These poems employ both exact rhyme and slant rhyme (sometimes called half rhyme or assonance). For instance, in the first poem, "Land Owner," the a-rhyming words, *work* and *talk*, are slant rhymes, while the b-rhyming words, *wage* and *sage*, are exact rhymes.

The traditional metrical (or rhythmic) form underlying most of the poems is iambic pentameter, which is the most common poetic meter in the English language. One way to remember what it sounds like is by speaking this line: "The rain in Spain falls mainly on the plain." If you say it four or five times, you'll have the regular beat the lines are built on. In this line the rhyming words are all accented. Since a too regular beat quickly becomes boring, I've added several little grace notes, unaccented syllables, to most of the lines, in order to roughen up, or syncopate, the rhythm. It's as if I'd done this to that rain-in-Spain line: "Does the rain in her Spain still fall mainly on his windowpane?" Again, looking at the first poem in the book, the first line could easily be a regular iambic pentameter line, like this: "There's nothing shameful in good, honest work." Say that line out loud a couple of times. And then read the line as it stands in the poem: "There ain't nothing shameful about good, honest work." Can you hear the grace notes, the syncopated, more playful rhythm? You should be able to hear that syncopation in many of the poems in this book.

No poet wants to keep writing the same form over and over. Part of the pleasure the poet receives from composing the poem comes from playfulness and discovery. Perhaps you can recognize the games I played with the rhymes as I wrote some of the poems. "African Mutual Relief Society," for instance. The little sermon in that poem, by the way, is based on the Parable of the Talents, Matthew 25:14–30; Luke 19:12–28. Perhaps you'll enjoy noticing the variations in the rhyme schemes I used in "Wild Night" and "Professor Hesser, Music Lessons."

All of the poems written in the voice of Matilda Polk are written in a form—I call it the "Tildie"—I invented for this speaker.

"The Park Theatre" and "The Shakespeare Riot" are both written in lines whose rhythm is a bit more regular than most of the other poems in the book. Since both of them refer to the plays of William Shakespeare, they imitate the unrhymed iambic pentameter lines, or blank verse, in which his plays are written.

Several poems in this book are sonnets. A sonnet is a 14-line poem that usually rhymes in some way. "Address" and "Babylon" are unusual sonnets because they are terza rima sonnets. Terza rima is poetry written in three-line stanzas (or "tercets") with interlinked end rhymes. The rhymes follow this pattern: aba, bcb, cdc, ded, efe, etc. This ancient form was first used by Dante Alighieri in his *Divine Comedy*, and he was followed by other Italian poets of the Renaissance, like Boccaccio and Petrarch. Thomas Wyatt and Geoffrey Chaucer brought terza rima into English poetry in the fouteenth century; Romantic poets including Byron and Shelley used it in the nineteenth century. By the way, the contents of both "Address" and "Babylon" are taken from the published speeches of the nineteenth-century abolitionist Mrs. Maria W. Stewart.

"Counting Blessings" is intended to sound like an Irish jig, when it is spoken aloud.

"Thompson and Seaman Vows, African Union Church" imitates the form of the wedding announcements published in the Sunday *New York Times* society pages.

"New York to Nicaragua" is the first of several poems in which I experimented with a new kind of "rhyme," which I came across several years ago in the work of American poet William Meredith (1919–2007). I don't know if Meredith had a name for it, but I call it "conceptual rhyme." I used conceptual rhyme in some poems in one of my earlier books, but I pushed the experiment a little bit further here. If rhyme is a sort of "echo" of sound (man/can) or sight (slaughter and laughter), conceptual rhyme "echoes" related intellectual concepts. In "New York to Nicaragua," "sky" is rhymed conceptually by echoing related concepts: "sunsets," "stars," and "moonlight." In "Nicaragua Crossing," "del Sur," "San Juan," "el Castillo," and "Cocibolca" are rhymed conceptually, related because they are all Spanish words. In "Sisters of Charity," the a-rhymes of each stanza are conceptually related by being opposites: "day/night," " more/less," "poor/rich," "nuns/tarts," and "slaves/home."

In "Make-Believe," instead of alternating sound rhymes and conceptual rhymes, I combined them in tercets which incorporate two kinds of rhyme: a conceptual rhyme and a sound rhyme. So in the first stanza, "slave/free" is a conceptual rhyme because the words are opposites, and the next line rhymes with a sound rhyme: "free/Legree." In the second stanza a conceptual rhyme of opposites—"whip/"embrace"—goes on to a sound rhyme —"embrace/race." Each of the four stanzas of this poem rhymes in this manner.

In "Sleep-Out," each quatrain contains three end words that are conceptual rhymes, and one word that doesn't rhyme with the rest at all.

"Pig on the Ice" is an Italian, or Petrarchan, sonnet.

"The Law of Eminent Domain" is a "found poem," composed of phrases lifted whole from the actual law of eminent domain of the state of New York.

Poets are interested in stuff like this. Maybe you'll find it interesting, too!

—*Marilyn Nelson*